to be continued

to be continued

ANNE BLONSTEIN

Shearsman Books

First published in the United Kingdom in 2011 by
Shearsman Books Ltd
58 Velwell Road
Exeter EX4 4LD

www.shearsman.com

ISBN 978-1-84861-173-3

Acknowledgements

Grateful acknowledgement is made to the editors of the following
publications in which poems from this collection, sometimes in slightly
different versions, first appeared:
Borderlands ('green'), *Lilith* ('structure of return (ii)'), *Orbis* ('structure of
return (i)'), *Osiris* ('because we know the same things but', 'towards an
aesthetics of', 'woman in a green satin dress'), *Pearl* ('the tram'), *Poetry
Salzburg Review* ('through the ephemeral bonds above'), *Switchback* ('to
thing to thing from thing'), *Tears in the Fence* ('the unperformed meeting
of refuse and zoologicality'), *Tiger's Eye* ('they gave them the names of
saints', 'what are they called i asked', 'footsteps coming through snow'),
Tremblestone ('when a freshwater pearl bracelet', 'an imperfect world'),
Wisconsin Review ('fin-de-siècle dream for sibylle').

'thou shalt not kill' was first printed as part of the Dusie Wee-Chap project.

Contents

mistress of the crazy chromosome

to be continued

to be continued

mistress of the crazy chromosome

actor

(famous) he agrees to meet her
(sleepless) in a quiet italian restaurant
on another continent (imagination)
while billie holiday sings

"solitude"

she offers him a dreamplay
a love story locked in a box
in the archives of a library
bombed while they whisper

when a freshwater pearl bracelet

she fiddled with
like a rosary
or other beads
whose silky milkiness suggested
the teeth of baby angels
or the calcified tears of ghosts

broke

one strand of a living
between purchase and a loose description failed
contacts to those epidermal receptors amplifying
inaudibles from the past

between

the translated shadows of girls
brought by poverty into cities
to service men and women
domestically and sexually
sacrificing future tenses for unconditional modes of the present

and

the ache of accentuated muscles
the apostrophic smoke of a french cigarette
the echo of a hawk's wings
a residue of ambergris

an imperfect world

in which the 12th-century japanese poet finds
the synthetic silk sleeves of her chrysanthemum
and banana-leaved 'made in switzerland' kimono
won't absorb the tears she sheds watching

assassinations

genocides and deforestations on television
while her 21st-century pillow-friend dreams
of butterflies falling off the ceiling
cracked blue glass bowls

the unperformed meeting of refuse and zoologicality

having fled germany for norway in 1937
kurt schwitters
finally arrived
in england
which interned him as an enemy alien
granting him citizenship

in 1948
he

had died two days before
in ambleside dreaming of anemones and nasturtiums
an unsingable necklace for the swan
that swallowed his watch

the red roofs of tsingtao
for f.-l.s.

scratched by sea-salt
that deposits an untranscribable
tang
in its beer

like a peacock's memory

a six-year-old girl
building sand-temples hears her father's voice
unfold from waves mauver than explaining
their rate of displacement

they gave them the names of saints

when a hot tamarisk-scented wind
carried echoes upstream
between her legs
from unsatisfied deserts
over the cataracts of mistake

to an orphan brother
kneeling

in sand resharpening memory's arrows
exactly — while she caressed boundless black curls -
tomorrow they must bury a friendship
with her copper mirror

if

for thomas

i wove you a tapestry
warped with transfusion-red tubes
wefted in nile-blue cottons thinner than
breaking
and an uncompromising

golden thread
from another conversation

would you hang it perhaps
in the fifth chamber of your heart
where one daughter synthesizes painless silks
the other repairs scrolls?

when night steals her sleep

and her dreams
do the mafia angels
pay a good price on the roseblack market
for their rhythms and unfinished
choices? do they

watch a conductor scratch the air

with a splinter of bone
harmony haunted by a suspended russian lament
as his left hand grasps saltchords
whispered by drowning men

green

velvet trousers
for a journey through a painting by max ernst
in the company of refugees from darfur
and simone weil's cat
(if she had one)

— a lonely music covers the horizon —

for transcriptions of their curves
to attempt before a gondola floats again
on the unhealthy waters of memory
smuggling florentines to jerusalem

through the ephemeral bonds above

the dancefloor
bodies orbit
other bodies

in a radical silence
the music cannot reduce

when a cell must die
it floods itself with reactive oxygen species
it tears its chromosomes to pieces
it forgets how to listen

to thing to thing from thing

prepositions fell off verbs
and now fly around this language
like post-gnostic angels

a marxist-red paperclip
reassures the unpaid bills

she in a laced metaphor
his endings tailored off at unexposed borders
the divorce between up and on
made out a twentieth century

fin-de-siècle dream for sibylle

in a lecture theatre
a presentation of your thesis
by an actor and actress
before a screen of images
so complex and aesthetic
half the audience scramble out

while the rest of us
enter a city

whose signs you have disprepared
and i struggle to remove lace gloves
but promise his persistence a dance
if he guesses my name

dancer

partnered in each city
of a multilingual programme

by spanish shadows
choreographing german sentences
with unanticipated endings

perhaps he could grip english
around the wrists and slide her between
romance and the security of grammar
polarizing a body's lyric orthodoxies

because we know the same things but
for c.l.

differently
and for once
unadorned words
and unadulterated syntax
appear adequate
to apprehension —
the angels need not take off their wings

for this party
i've donned a skirt of mirrors

bring her an amber heart
eyes forgetting how to crystallize the dark
and fingers that want to dance
over the edge of purple

structure of return (i)

to a daily bike ride
up the trumpington road
from bedsit to laboratory
through mist and exhaust fumes
past the school whose teachers told

jean rhys
her voice would never sell
lace lingerie

in harrods (one could imagine)
the dolphins on the food hall tiles
leaping through sappho's broken lips {   } kiss
salty foam from her fingertips

i imagine him

gathering driftwood and shells
watching the sky teach pink
while he wrote poems in the sand
to be read and adsorbed
by pacific salts

returning to a cluttered pinewood table
and storm lamp

typing letters to new york
ritually sipping the burgundy bonds between chivalry
and heresy while the nightmoths danced
a farewell to wedding dresses

both had gardens beside the sea

and while one cultivated pale green dragons
in the hearts of his aubergines
the other painted the spines on his thistles
every shade of blue
and grey

until he could no longer see
the naked ghosts

huddle around the chanukah candles
stain the shadows with a salt tang
in the silence after the music
no resurrection but in dreams

structure of return (ii)

like god
to his throne in the clouds
chuckling
because his rabbis have outwitted him
in a debate

or at least that's how
the rabbis tell the story

their wives in the kitchen
know the joke was in the knots
they tied in the soup noodles
he swallowed 3000 years later

angel above lac leman

with george byron's heart
eyes phylogenized from cloud
in the angle of each wing beat
a devastated sigh
crystallizing into a moonflake of time

(our poliverse gestates through the text
our dreams extravagate possibilities)

he stuck the angel's feathers
into a satin duvet caressed by shadows
when he opened the pill bottle
the pink sounded like sea

like a leaf falling on its shadow

each death meets the birth that made it possible
each hand caressing petal or cheek
closes time
and will remember antigone's
guiding her father
over tragedy's horizon

ask her the colour of the clouds :
peached — prayer — passionately

uniqueness has a cosmic sense
of humour where piano notes sneak past
curly pubic hairs into a passage
fugued by instead and lymphocyte

migrnation
for cecilia

there is no border
the israeli soldier said in the film
because there is
no palestinian state
there are no borders
the jewished poet writes in a poem

as she takes a barb from the wire
to scratch

into her skin six zeros
that numberless number discovered by the other
for the dead to walk through
walls smooth as an olive's

what are they called i asked

the smiling florist
of the dark-red-blurring-into-white
roses

i was buying
"lipstick"
she replied
and we both laughed
(embarrassed

by images of disappointed women)
the gentleman she had served before me
was blind and friday-evening talkative —
my roses have no fragrance

footsteps coming through snow

those of a blackbird
those of a doe
too frightened to watch
bodies falling against their

breath
(her father sang songs
in yiddish polish hebrew
and french

but screamed in the night
watching his son his daughter his wife
turn to listen to his heart)
below the story of white

promises promises

place the tear

of a child whose best friend
has been killed
by soldiers
or terrorists

in a green contact lens
and let it evaporate to dryness : place
the contact lens on your eye
and read the scratches scratches

towards an aesthetics of

might one call it
attraction
when the air between two bodies
thins

when the words
— oh such innocent questions —
dance like iridescent bubbles
then burst

the psychology of an axis
about which a self-mocking smile spins
better studied in a dream vineyard
than a classroom of hope

the tram

was full of english-speaking employees
and visitors to the city
i hid my tongue
by reading a novel in french
a swiss drunk

turned to a passenger with an irish accent
to ask slowly
and syntactfully :

"can you tell me young
man — how to dismantle an atomic bomb?"
others descended at the wrong stop
heedless of his good advice

structure of return (iii)

to a dream's end several nights ago
in which wasps
detached themselves from a wall
and swarmed through the gap
between my collar and back

five days ago
the poet-fool
thomas kling
died
aged 47
from cancer

the newspaper journalist writes about
experiencing the sensual materiality of this textbody
eyes looping algorithmically through light-suras
and always again — "die Wespe"

woman in a green satin dress

walks through a field of
where there should have been wheat ears
tiny white skulls
which rattle and chatter
advising her to find
the confluence of stories

law and love
tumble in washing machines
until they're too expensive to repair

in the eye of language
all the letters lost and not yet
imagined fall away from the light
created before heaven and earth

thou shalt not kill

exodus 20 : 13

לא תרצח   ס

for susana gardner

lilaced
  & anemoned

  tissue of
rain-stippled
        hemitheses

   exyoudating

*

  a line approaches

   to record
a starling's   heartbeat

    :

   experimetrical

*

  lady away

   throws rhythms
    straggle   her

  exactness

live anon

   in a tremble-
       roomed
story   (house

   expositioned

*

lost in   attention

   to repetitions
      store holes

or   exclusions

*

   letting an alphabet

    transfuse a requisite of
    starcelled
    haemoglobal

   exceptors

a lot of   ashes

   too rich in
      stifles here

  excendiary

*

  litanies of autonomy :

   a thin river of stillness
   heard

     exortations

*

  lemonmoth
airweaving

  through
    a reality-
stringed
     harp

exstaltic

lust agendas —

    tonight a row
startles   —   a hand

    explanes

*

    in a lattice of after

    thoughts
r( )membering
      structures
     a high

    exsit(e)ability

*

    of leaves of (almost)

    a text ramifies along a
      cedar-haunted

    support

littoralize (abrasions)

    a trail of redshanks across
    a sanded heartscape

       shorewords

*

lazy   (attentive)

    at a table's   rim
      circadian heretiquettes

    shelled

*

    late (anaesthetized)

       thickness restoring
seen-
     hungry

    secrets

learning   (in abeyance)

   to reason in a
      civilian hospital

    sacro(   )ligiously

*

lightscorded
  (in all

. . . tenebral . . .
(or recursivity
of a singable
    horizonless

   (scale

*

  loopflowers (anemophilous)

    in their roots
       cicadian hesitations

   sostenuto

lips (air)

   twisting remnants of
           song
around his

    spine

*

least (apart)

or
a treatise on   rapport
or
    a city hermit

or
        shakeholding

*

last   (adagio)

of tonight   — riddlelike
symphonied   —   a hand

    spanned

in a language of (aerated   )

tropically
routed
cerebrals
hydrolysed

s   tabil   i   ties

*

)lunarity :(

touchwide   reproducing
   a time-
 spasmed
            haemorrhaging

      space

*

lords and "   "

  a terrestrial record of
"timeseeded   "
 "   hollowscened"

      sediments

lacy {   }

toughness of a
    reform
        timesilking her

   subject

*

lexicells ○

   transporting responses   ○
in a timesalted   ○
   heterotypic

○   solute

*

legacy

to
     recovered in
   a timeskin
how-

   -sutured

. . . laevonotation

      two recrystallizing
    time-
saturated hopes

saturated . .   ?

*

(— laminar

  or turbulent
rush
    or a timesuckled
    hushed

   specificity ?)

*

lyrischism

   troubadour & residents
timesighting
     a harmonic

  signature

» luminalsense «

tender a rose
    of timesorbent
    hot

surfaces

*

less

tonight
rests in
    timeshy
    a hand

sines :

11 august – 11 september 2006

to be continued

for sam

«so much tenderness»

begins *keeping space lighter into violet*

i forgot my middle name
i forgot the differential equation of zero
i forgot to say thank you
i found a touched by hidden structures

«*brighter*»

even though our bodies are not stars
kabbalists saw luminous vessels

break · collapsing into their restraint
what the poetess promised to the yogi
when his breath was dream hot
these words spin through a burnt map

«contact»

and if i could etch my contours with
yours into the nocturnal sky *knowing*
skinny lines intimate vastnesses —

      but the stratosphere is freezing
while your body releases bonds into heat
that my fingers remember : deep surfaces
      guiding proofs of a work in progress

«to be continued»

because we were not meant to be continued · the full
moon shot from the heavens (*kaddish slipped lipwards
into waiting*

                        to mingle tradition with innovation
              syncopate laughter smiles and tears into bodies
                    cantillated by a smothered legacy :) can
you improvise this —— ^{grace} —— note sustaining your line …

«*although she's not, she's still there*»

she's tracing triangles in the air · with salt ·
with the secrets of their future · and softer than
syllables *kisses sculpted like withouts* ·

the imprints of your body
defies the abstractions of time · like dreamscapes
that never fade from inner screens
she feels your geometries written into mine

«to the sea»

and to the hand that will hold mine · take me
up to the sea that saved my family — and
drowned their history · *kelp segues littoral
waterscores* ·

    my grandfather forbade my grandmother
who sold singer sewing machines in selfridges
    from swimming across the channel · legs
legs legs legs (membering a french inheritance)

«*endless over this small universe*»

having just lit the first of thirty-six
candles · blood-red · it flickers in another
room · i sip a dry martini · twist my curls ·
kaleidoscope ~ sand ~ letters ~ wants ~

       the questions i cannot ask
dive below the surface of your poems ~
       if they find splits and corals
will bracelet them with her winter follicles

« »

romanticism she abandoned in a
room   postered   by   premature
muses   ·   sentimentally   she
translates without touching it · and
the   only   part   of   nostalgia   she
recognizes : the first syllable *keeps*
space   lyrically   viable   —

perhaps the most important word
        in your sea poems is the one
you overlooked · or lost · or threw
    into the yellow waves of the past

«*sometimes colouring again bright blue*»

if (*time bubbles through*)

you are in the air
and i vibrate at an ultraslow wavelength
perhaps you will feel my curves
wrap their intervals around your reactive bonds

«*surrounded by skinless water*»

i am raining myselves into your dreams . . .
togethered by trains

each line squiggles unpredictably northwords
depositing a trail of dust onto
the read-hot glass of memory
cracks — i am pouring into your hands

«open mond»

all the things we did not have to say because
all the things we do not have that say *tissue
bodies' thesauruses*

　　　　　little but by little but
we could build the school of ampersand
　　　with cracks in the mortal though
so : the moonlight can translate your smile

«more fragile than a mouse, more thin»

sudan to january · salted red pepper with
rosehip tea · and phrases that returned
from the past along the edges of bat
wings · wittgenstein's niece *tenders
breathweathered thoughts* :

"who · if not you?" not
in never falling · "when · if not now?"
but in flying from each fall
toenails painted with soot and open eyes

«from the dreamscape»

an owl landed here : *she brought · tonight*

in our kitchen i grind
anxieties · almonds · and an absence of allegro ·
sprinkle them over an unspoken conversation ·
you will find feathers in the refrigerator

«surrendering»

to possibilities indubitably takes off her
white cotton underwear · *shivers because
tomorrow*

                    the space that must play
the green and yellow echoes of development
during the weeks of their separunion
stretches a slowed skin around an internity

«*not totally yet, also some*»

because we have not found how our blood
will get into the orange · *shadows bite time*

because · if our love is
more like fruit salad than champagne or
an english breakfast · what untasted colours
will you mix into my dreaming flesh?

«inside red rubber surface to warm skin»

perhaps the water has turned to as night-
fast a blue as the indigo patterns on the
cloth miriam wrapped moses in *shyness
bursts totality*

like starseeds in the vacuum
as the water cools and slim figures
of unformulized curves and open angles
are shed into the absense · and reabsorbed

«differences though seem (still)»

she knows (now) that she will have to learn
· (slowly) · how to caress all the shades of
your spaces · or even bless them with new
names : *shimmergent* · *bluminal* ·
tantrigenic ·

how to · weigh a second
how to · wash poems in the dark
how to unwrap · a grey heart
(because she's spinning · a postulate of me)

«*stately old ladies*»

three of them · *appropriating dream's reason*

before the light forgets possibilities
spinoza's mother dances in smoke-grey silks
anne frank performs an unwritten script
and the future massages your fingertips (

«energy»

from within the work of between · facultative
structures *alternate dreamwide restrictions*

after the snow has melted
(but will the inheritors of our world
perceive the semanticized nature translating me
your exsited breath and each seagull's scream?)

«bevestigt de ander per definitie allen zichzelf?»

today esther rides out of the story on
a bicycle wreathed in violet crocuses
anticipating dreambridged routes

i would like to string
my smiles along a crack in time
that you might construct a light
to suspend between night and your body

«you have a good memory»

of your naked body sitting into mine sat last
night in a slightly lumpy armchair at the
brockenhaus concert
    absorbing dreamcontrasted rhythms

              your bed calls to me
and the discomposed arrangements of the sea
        break a restless thought over *klagen* :
            i can not to you *assai lento*

«your preciseness in language»

who once measured pebbles on a beach ·
as if to demonstrate physical laws · now
the currents in her head carry crimes
further   than   natural   philosophy
antisatisfying dreamless rules

i would like to dive
into the sky with you · shadowfast · bring
the unread weight of our kisses
to the most silent among the angels

«intense»

when i can hold your posture once
again and · faithful to my translation ·
proposition it between heine and jabès
· when lips have passed the border
looping   pain   through   presence
authenticating dreamt reciprocals

          the kiss that surprised you
returns to us wrapped in a question :
          what order of poem is this
if i paint every orifice with chocolate?

«with all our dreams!»

with all our differences *now joins sign &*
narratability

in a house of unfolding
where the light splits into coloured walls
passing through history · heartbeats · happiness · her
desire twirls in a ballgown of dust